Counting Books

3,2,1 Go!

A Transportation Countdown

by **Sarah L. Schuette**

Reading Consultant:
Jennifer Norford
Senior Consultant
Mid-continent Research
for Education and Learning

Capstone
press

Mankato, Minnesota

A+ Books are published by Capstone Press
P.O. Box 669, 151 Good Counsel Drive, Mankato, Minnesota 56002
http://www.capstonepress.com

1 2 3 4 5 6 08 07 06 05 04 03

Library of Congress Cataloging-in-Publication Data
Schuette, Sarah L., 1976–
    3,2,1 go!: a transportation countdown / by Sarah L. Schuette.
    p. cm.—(Counting books)
    Summary: Counts backward from ten to one starting with ten school buses and ending with
one city bus.
    Includes bibliographical references and index.
    ISBN 0-7368-1678-X (hardcover) ISBN 0-7368-9478-0 (paperback)
    1. Motor vehicles—Juvenile literature. 2. Transportation—Juvenile literature.
3. Counting—Juvenile literature. [1. Motor vehicles. 2. Vehicles. 3. Transportation. 4. Counting.]
I. Title: Three, two, one go. II. Title. III. Series.
TL147 .S386 2003
629.22—dc21   2002015886

Credits
Jason Knudson, designer; Gary Sundermeyer, photographer

Note to Parents, Teachers, and Librarians
3,2,1 Go! uses color photographs and a nonfiction format to introduce children
to various modes of transportation while building mastery of basic counting skills.
It is designed to be read aloud to a pre-reader or to be read independently by an
early reader. The images help early readers and listeners understand the text
and concepts discussed. The book encourages further learning by including
the following sections: Words to Know, Read More, Internet Sites, and Index.
Early readers may need assistance using these features.

How many toys sit on the shelf?

10

TEN toy school buses

School buses take children to and from school.

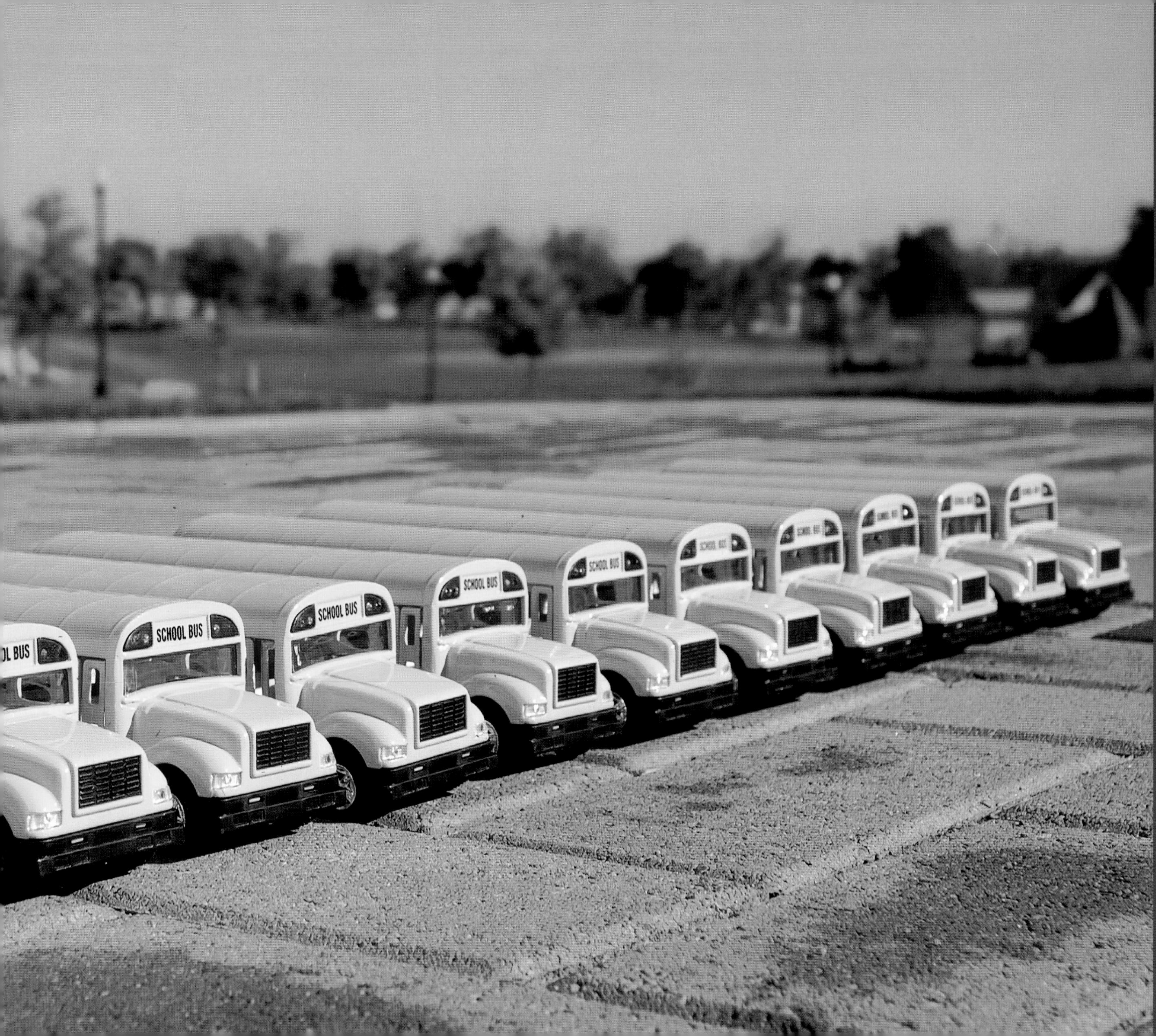

10
9
8
7
6
5
4
3
2
1
0

NINE toy ambulances

Ambulances hurry to accidents.

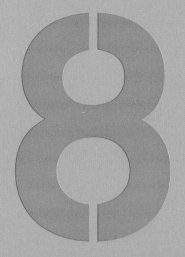

EIGHT toy train cars

Train cars travel on railroad tracks.

7

SEVEN toy police cars

Police officers travel in police cars to keep towns and cities safe.

6

SIX toy airplanes

Airplanes can soar in the sky.

9
8
7
6
5
4
3
2
1
0

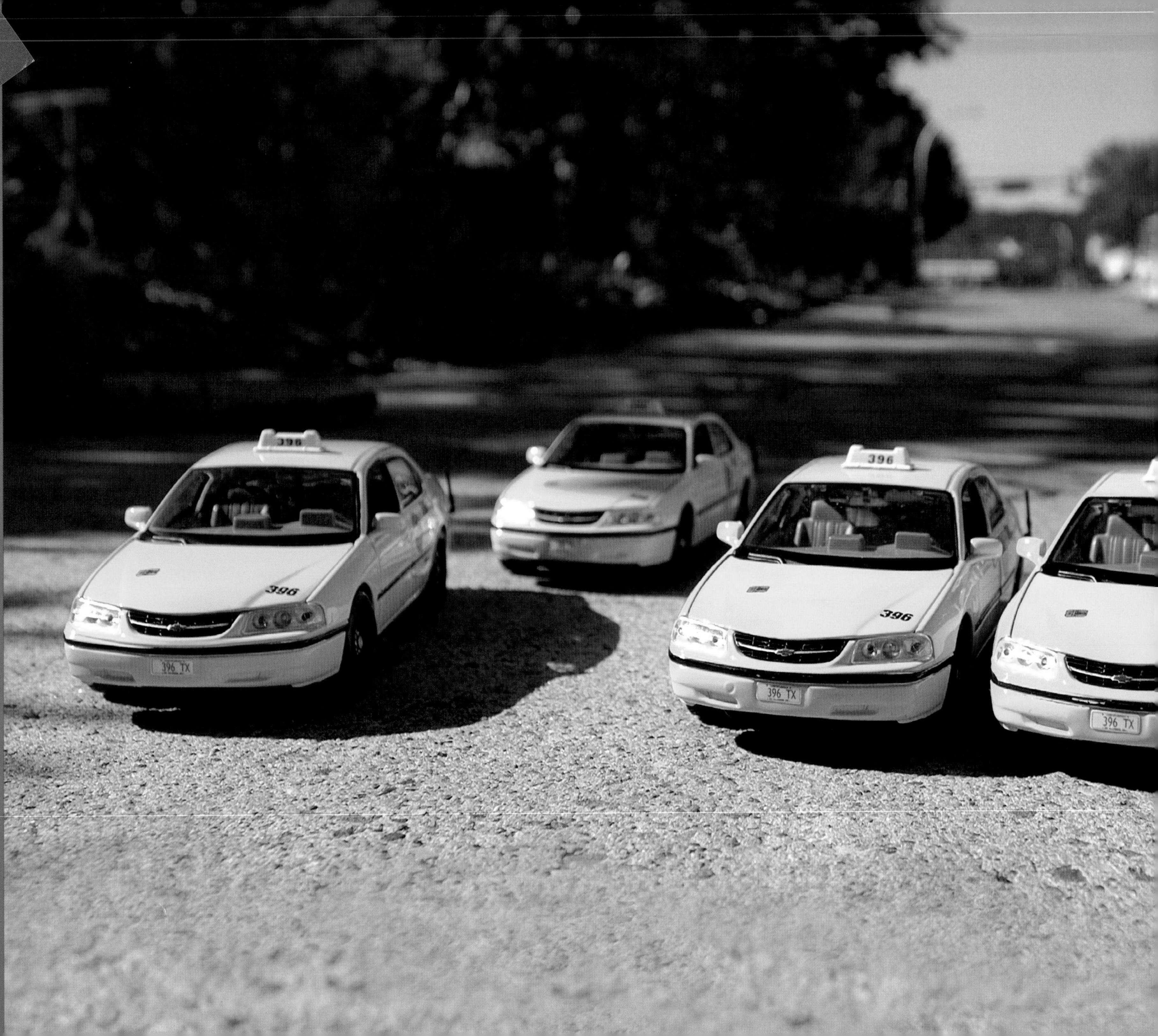

5

FIVE toy taxicabs

People ride around town in taxicabs.

15

4

FOUR toy tugboats

Tugboats pull barges in the water.

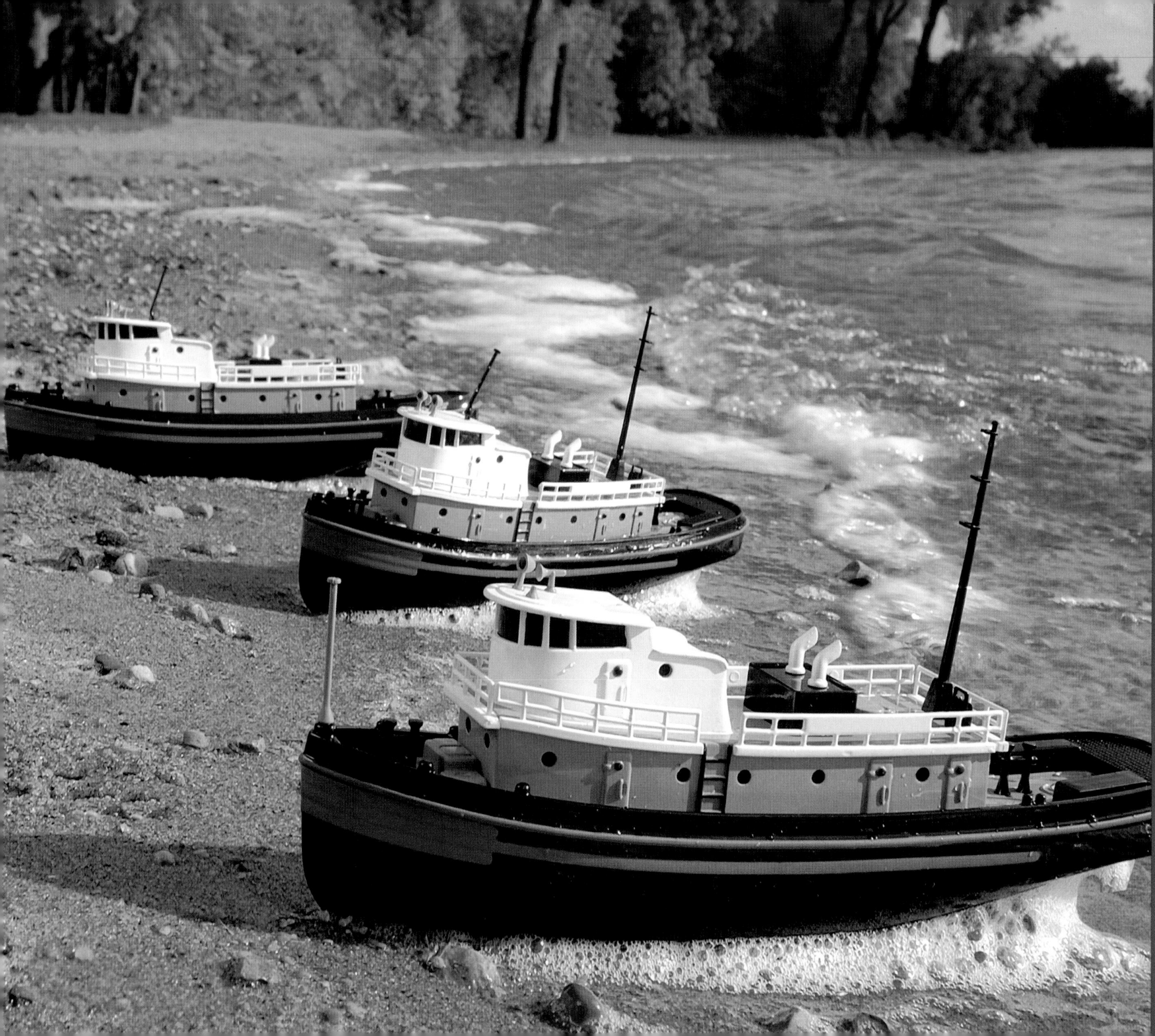

10
9
8
7
6
5
4
3
2
1
0

THREE toy dairy trucks

Dairy trucks deliver milk.

2

TWO toy fire trucks

Firefighters ride in fire trucks.

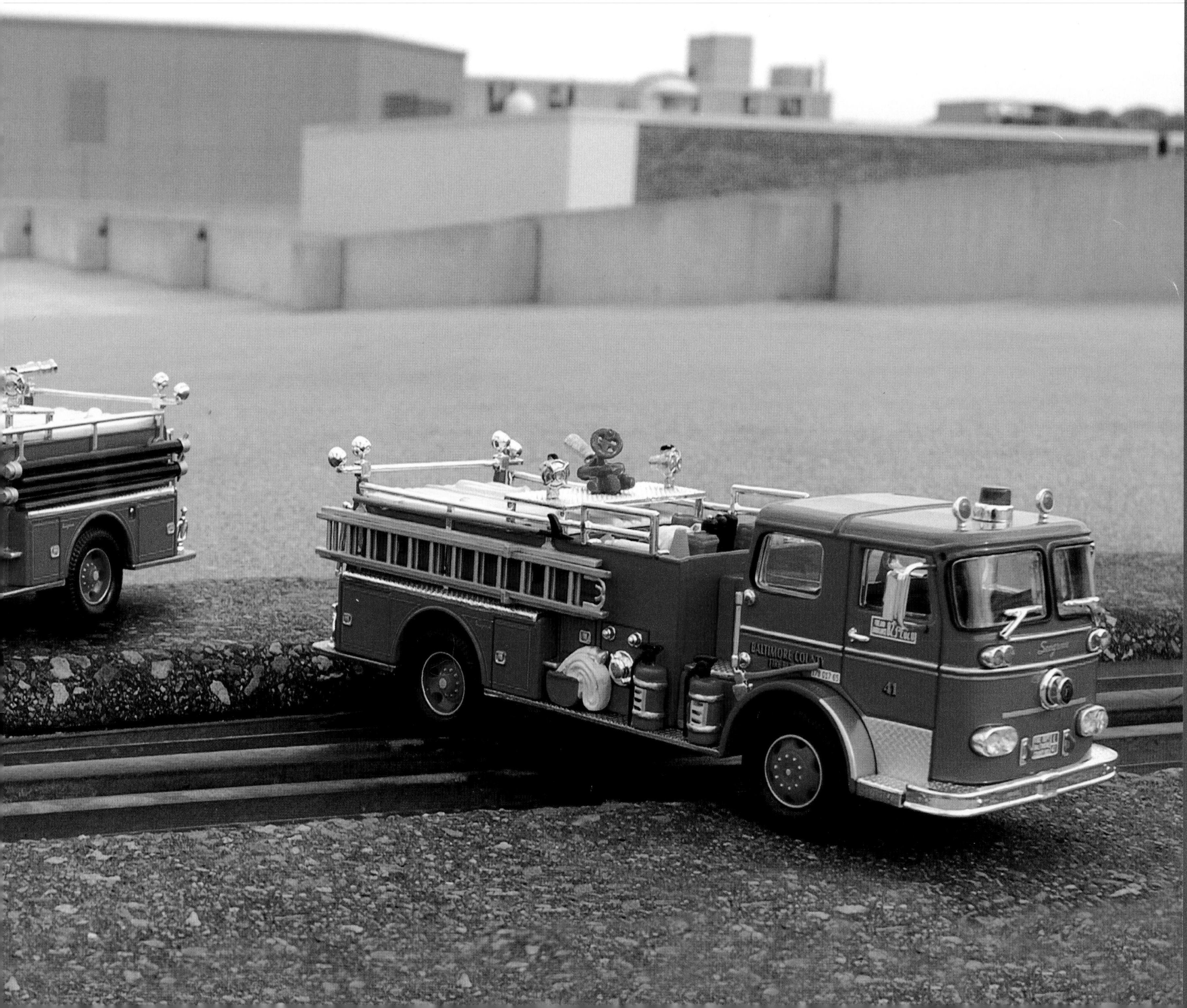

10
9
8
7
6
5
4
3
2
1
0

CITY TRANSIT AUTHORITY

6947

ONE toy city bus

A city bus carries passengers around a city.

How many toys have wheels?

How many toys have wings?

How many toys can float?

Things That Go

school bus

ambulance

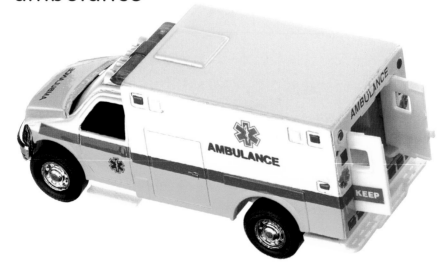

tugboat

dairy truck

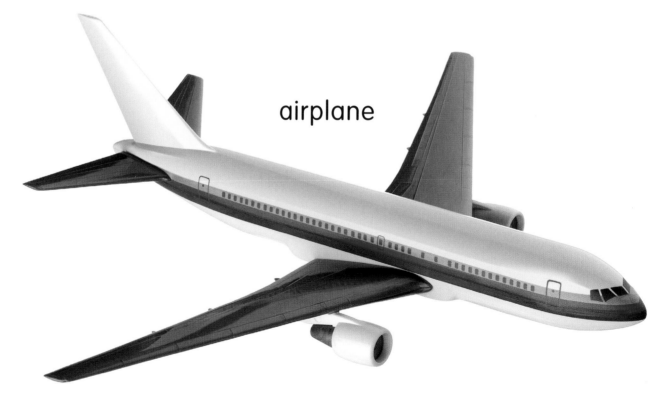

airplane

police car

train

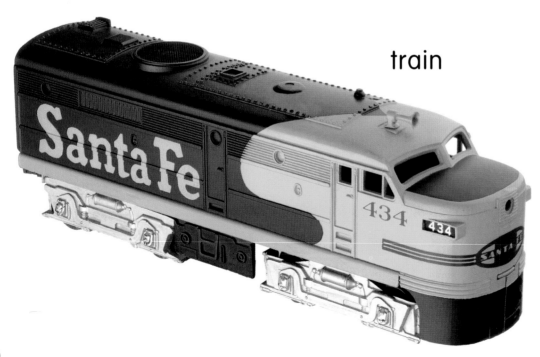

fire truck

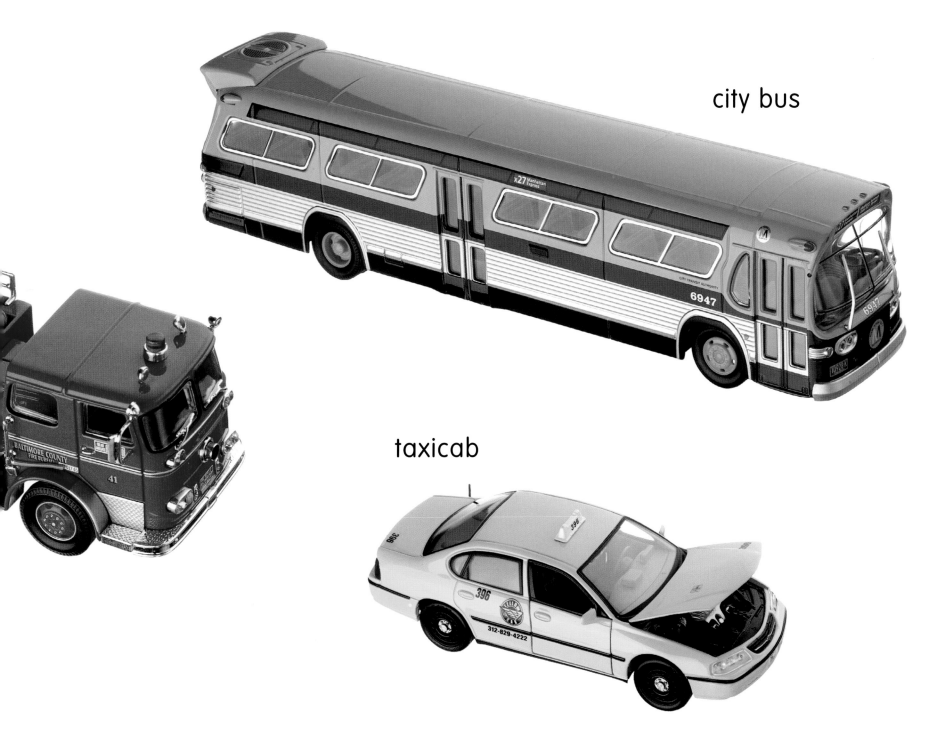

city bus

taxicab

29

Words to Know

accident (AK-si-duhnt)—something that takes place unexpectedly and that often involves people being hurt

barge (BARJ)—a long boat with a flat bottom; barges carry heavy cargo from place to place; barges are pulled by tugboats because they cannot move by themselves.

dairy (DAIR-ee)—a product made with milk; milk, cheese, and yogurt are dairy products.

officer (OF-uh-sur)—someone who is in charge of other people; police officers are in charge of people's safety

passenger (PASS-uhn-jur)—someone besides the driver who travels in a vehicle; passengers ride in taxicabs, buses, and airplanes.

soar (SOR)—to fly high in the air

Read More

Carter, Don. *Get to Work, Trucks!* Brookfield, Conn.: Roaring Brook Press, 2002.

Nathan, Emma. *Transportation.* Eyeopeners Series. San Diego, Calif.: Blackbirch Press, 2003.

Schaefer, Lola M. *Wheels, Wings, and Water ABC.* Chicago: Heinemann Library, 2003.

Signore, Derek. *Counting Road Signs.* Hampton, Ga.: Southern Charm Press, 2002.

Internet Sites

Track down many sites about transportation.

Visit the FACT HOUND at *http://www.facthound.com*

IT IS EASY! IT IS FUN!
1) Go to *http://www.facthound.com*
2) Type in: 073681678X
3) Click on "FETCH IT" and FACT HOUND will find several links hand-picked by our editors.

Relax and let our pal FACT HOUND do the research for you!

Index